REMARKABLE REPTILES

SNAKES

James E. Gerholdt

Published by Abdo & Daughters, 4940 Viking Drive, Suite 622, Edina, Minnesota 55435.

Library bound edition distributed by Rockbottom Books, Pentagon Tower, P.O. Box 36036, Minneapolis, Minnesota 55435.

Copyright © 1994 by Abdo Consulting Group, Inc., Pentagon Tower, P.O. Box 36036, Minneapolis, Minnesota 55435 USA. International copyrights reserved in all countries. No part of this book may be reproduced in any form without written permission from the publisher.

Printed in the United States.

Cover Photo credit: Peter Arnold
Interior Photo credits: James E. Gerholdt
Photos courtesy of Eric Thiss, pages 6, 12, 16

Edited By: Julie Berg

LIBRARY OF CONGRESS CATALOGING-IN-PUBLICATION DATA

Gerholdt, James E., 1943-
    Snakes / James E. Gerholdt.
        p.   cm. -- (Remarkable Reptiles)
    Includes glossary and index.
    ISBN 1-56239-307-3
    1. Snakes -- Juvenile Literature.   [1. Snakes.] I. Title.
    II. Series: Gerholdt, James E. 1943- Remarkable Reptiles.
QL666.06G27 1994
597.96--dc20   94-7795
                                                                  CIP
                                                                    AC

CONTENTS

SNAKES -- 4

SIZES -- 7

SHAPES -- 8

COLORS --- 10

HABITAT -- 13

SENSES --- 14

DEFENSE --- 17

FOOD -- 18

BABIES -- 20

GLOSSARY --- 22

INDEX --- 23

SNAKES

Snakes are reptiles. Reptiles are ectothermic. This means they get their body temperature from the environment, either from lying in the sun or on a warm rock or the warm ground. Snakes like temperatures from 75 to 85 degrees Fahrenheit, and some need it even warmer. If they get too hot, they will die and if they are too cool, their bodies won't work. There are more than 2,700 species of snakes. They are found almost everywhere in the world.

This Northern water snake looks odd because it has very few scales.

This Albino red-sided garter snake is from Kansas.

This Timber rattle-snake is sunning itself on a warm rock.

5

This Burmese python is about 8 feet long and may grow to 15 feet or longer.

SIZES

Some snakes are giants. The Anaconda from South America has been reported to reach a length of 37 1/2 feet. The reticulated python from Southeast Asia has been recorded at 33 feet, and the African rock python at 32 feet. The longest snake in the United States is the Eastern indigo. It can reach a length of almost 9 feet. Many snakes are not as large. The smallest snake in the world is the Brahminy blind snake. An adult is less than 6 inches long.

This Plains blind snake from Texas is the size of a toothpick.

SHAPES

Snakes come in many different shapes. Many are long and slender and some are short and fat. Most snakes have long tails, but others, like the boas and pythons, have short tails. And while a lot of snakes have long slender heads, others have triangle-shaped heads. But this does not mean they are venomous! Millions of years ago, snakes had legs, but not anymore. If you look closely at a boa or python you will see a pair of spurs where the tail starts. This is all that is left of their legs.

The Eastern hognose snake is short and fat.

The Blue racer is long and slender.

COLORS

Many snakes are very brightly colored. Some are all one color, and others have several different colors. Other snakes are shaded to help them blend in with their surroundings. This is called camouflage. Male and female snakes are all the same color. Sometimes a snake will have cloudy colors and blue eyes. This means it is getting ready to shed its skin. After about a week, the eyes and skin clear up and the snake rubs its nose and chin on a rock and crawls out of the old skin. This is called ecdysis. The new skin is bright and shiny.

This Texas longnose snake has several colors.

This Eastern indigo snake's eyes turn blue when it is about to shed its skin.

This Albino checkered garter snake has red eyes.

11

This Mottled rock rattlesnake from Texas lives in rocky areas.

HABITAT

Snakes live in all different kinds of habitats. Some, like the blind snakes, live underground. Many like rocky areas, where they can sun themselves and find shelter. Other types live in sandy deserts where they can bury themselves in the sand. Many species of snakes live in the trees or hide on the forest floor. Some snakes, like the sea snakes, spend their entire lives in the ocean and never do come ashore.

SENSES

Snakes only have 3 of the 5 senses as humans. They have very poor eyesight, and can see mostly movement. Snakes that are active at night have vertical pupils to help them see better in the dark. When it is dark, the pupils open up to let more light in. Snakes have no ears and can't hear. They can feel vibrations through bones in their lower jaws. Some, like the rattlesnakes, have heat sensing pits between their mouth and nostrils to help locate their prey. The most important part of a snake is its tongue. It uses it to smell.

The Sonoran lyre snake from Arizona has vertical pupils.

This albino Plains garter snake is using its pink tongue to smell.

The Eastern hognose snake will play dead.

This Texas coral snake has red and yellow stripes and is very venomous.

DEFENSE

Camouflage is the best way a snake defends itself against its enemies. If its enemy can't see it, it is safe. Snakes aren't very fast, so they can't slip away from danger very easily. The fastest snake, the black mamba, can only move 7 miles per hour. A rattlesnake will sound its rattle to scare an enemy away. Others, like the hognose, will look fierce, and if this doesn't work, will play dead. Some snakes have bright colors to scare away their enemies. The venomous coral snakes and the harmless milk snakes have the same bright colors, but not in the same order.

This Timber rattlesnake's rattle makes a loud buzzing sound.

FOOD

All snakes eat other animals, or sometimes the eggs of these animals. No snake has ever been known to eat fruits or vegetables! Small snakes like the smooth green snake eat insects and caterpillars. The redbelly snake eats slugs and snails. Many snakes eat mice and other rodents. Garter snakes eat fish and frogs while the Eastern hognose eats almost nothing but toads. The big pythons can eat things like antelope, deer and pigs. Anacondas have been known to sometimes eat caiman, a South American alligator.

This Timber rattlesnake from Minnesota is just starting to swallow a ground squirrel.

This Corn snake from Florida is almost finished swallowing a mouse.

BABIES

Most snakes hatch from eggs. The eggs are laid in holes in the ground or sometimes in rotten logs. Sometimes a number of snakes will lay their eggs in the same place. Some snakes, like the ringnecks, will lay only a few eggs, while some of the pythons can lay as many as 100 eggs. While most snakes pay no attention to their eggs, the pythons will incubate them, and the king cobra actually builds a nest. Other snakes, like the boas and rattlesnakes, give birth to live babies.

These Corn snake eggs are almost ready to hatch.

Here the baby Corn snakes have opened slits in the eggs.

And here is one of the baby Corn snakes.

21

GLOSSARY

Albino (al-BYE-no) - An animal without normal colors, often yellow or pink in reptiles.

Camouflage (KAM-o-flaj) - The ability to blend in with the surroundings.

Ecdysis (EK-di-sis) - The act of losing the old skin.

Ectothermic (ek-to-THER-mik) - Regulating body temperature from an outside source.

Environment (en-VIE-ron-ment) - Surroundings an animal lives in.

Habitat (HAB-e-tat) - An area an animal lives in.

Reptiles (REP-tiles) - Scaly skinned animals with backbones.

Species (SPEE-ses) - A kind or type.

Venomous (VEN-o-mus) - Having poison to kill its food.

Vertical (VER-ta-cal) - Up and down, not sideways.

Index

A

Anaconda 7, 18
Asia 7

B

babies 20
Boa 8
Brahminy blind snake 7

C

Cobra 20
color 10, 17
Coral snake 17

D

defense 17

E

eggs 18, 20
eyesight 14

G

Garter snake 18

H

Hognose snake 17, 18

L

legs 8

N

nest 20

R

Reticulated python 7, 8, 18
Rattlesnake 14, 17

S

South America 7, 18
spurs 8

T

tails 8
tongue 14

23

About the Author

Jim Gerholdt has been studying reptiles and amphibians for more than 40 years. He has presented lectures and displays throughout the state of Minnesota for 9 years. He is a founding member of the Minnesota Herpetological Society and is active in conservation issues involving reptiles and amphibians in India and Aruba, as well as Minnesota.

Photo by Tim Judy